THE EVOLUTION OF WILL SMITH

THE EVOLUTION OF WILL SMITH

JASPER RAVENWOOD

CONTENTS

Introduction

The persona of Will Smith, an actor, singer-songwriter, rapper, and producer, began to take shape when he was cast as Will in the American sitcom *The Fresh Prince of Bel-Air*, which premiered in 1990. From there, Smith's career skyrocketed, turning him from a charismatic TV star into a bona fide Hollywood icon. The success of films like *Bad Boys* (1995) and the *Men in Black* franchise (starting in 1997) cemented his status as a reliable and bankable brand in the entertainment industry.

Smith's career was marked by numerous high-concept studio films that showcased his versatility and undeniable star power. However, he also faced challenges with less successful films, often those with more complex scripts that pushed him as an actor. These challenging roles were fewer and farther between, as Smith navigated a landscape dominated by blockbuster expectations.

Following a series of box office flops, Smith's reputation began to wane. He transitioned from being a self-reliant, franchise-friendly star to a figure entwined in the political and social narratives of his projects. Today, as we reflect on his journey from "The Fresh Prince," we see the unexpected return of a more reflective and multifaceted Will Smith.

The Fresh Prince of Bel-Air was a groundbreaking show for many reasons, and its cast of characters played a significant role in its success. Before the sitcom aired, Will Smith was already known as a successful rapper performing under the name The Fresh Prince alongside DJ Jazzy Jeff as the duo DJ Jazzy Jeff & The Fresh Prince. His casting in the series, during the height of his musical career, was a stroke of genius. The role propelled Smith, then a 20-year-old musician and budding actor, into Hollywood.

Smith seamlessly transitioned from a beloved TV star to a bankable movie star, following the paths of predecessors like Michael J. Fox and Tom Hanks. However, unlike many of his peers, Smith's journey from movie star to one of the industry's brightest superstars was not universally embraced in the age of streaming.

Let's explore how *The Fresh Prince* evolved from sitcom stardom to commanding blockbuster films and the various strategies and challenges Smith faced to stay afloat in the competitive entertainment industry.

CHAPTER 1

Early Life and Career

Childhood and Family Background

Willard Carroll Smith Jr., known as Will Smith, was born on September 25, 1968, in West Philadelphia. His father, Willard Carroll Smith Sr., owned a refrigeration company, and his mother, Caroline, worked for the Philadelphia school board. Raised in a Baptist family, Smith attended Our Lady of Lourdes, a private Catholic elementary school. Despite the challenges of their time, Smith's family maintained a middle-class lifestyle and upheld strict disciplinary methods, with punishment limited to confinement rather than corporal measures.

Smith's early exposure to entertainment came from his grandmother, Ellen Holloway, an opera singer who was highly respected in a predominantly white society. His father, a hardworking entrepreneur, and his mother, an administrative assistant, provided a supportive and stable environment. In his leisure time, young Will enjoyed watching animated shows and movies, planting the seeds of his desire to become a showman or actor.

Rise to Fame on *The Fresh Prince of Bel-Air*

Will Smith's foray into the entertainment industry began with his partnership with DJ Jazzy Jeff. Between 1987 and 1989, the duo dominated the record charts, earning the first Grammy awarded in the Rap category for their hit song "Parents Just Don't Understand" in 1989. Despite his strict Catholic upbringing and contentment with local success, Smith's journey took a pivotal turn at age 21.

At a party, a woman he danced with remarked that he was "cute but never going to make it in hip-hop because you're just so corny." This comment lingered with Smith. A week later, he learned that NBC, at the request of Renaissance Man Quincy Jones, was looking to turn the comedy "The Fresh Prince of Bel-Air" into a television show. Without the need for an audition, Smith was asked if he could act, to which he confidently replied, "Uh, probably. Who can tell me otherwise?" This role catapulted him into a household name.

The *Fresh Prince of Bel-Air* premiered in 1990, quickly becoming a beloved series that would define an era. Smith's charismatic portrayal of a street-smart teenager from Philadelphia navigating life in a wealthy Los Angeles neighborhood resonated with audiences. The show's success was not just a testament to Smith's talent but also a reflection of his real-life transition from Philadelphia to the glitz and glamour of Hollywood.

Despite early success, Smith faced financial turmoil due to poor financial management, finding himself millions in debt after a string of hits and the action bomb *Six Degrees of Separation*. The U.S. Internal Revenue Service launched a lawsuit, resulting in a substantial seizure of his assets. Smith worked diligently to repay his estimated $15 million debt, demonstrating his strong work ethic.

Through it all, *The Fresh Prince of Bel-Air* ran from 1990 to 1996, solidifying Smith's status in the entertainment industry. NBC's universal acclaim for the show opened doors for Smith, who evolved from a fresh-faced sitcom star to a man ready for blockbuster fame. Willard Carroll Smith Jr. had truly arrived, embracing his role as a superstar.

CHAPTER 2

Transition to Film

Following his success on television, Will Smith made a significant transition to film in the early 1990s. His breakout role in *Men in Black* (1997) earned him widespread acclaim, establishing the movie as the first in a highly successful franchise. That same year, Smith's powerful performance in the drama *The Pursuit of Happyness* garnered him an Academy Award nomination for Best Actor. By 2008, Forbes had ranked Smith as the most bankable star worldwide. By 2014, 17 of the 21 films in which Smith had played leading roles amassed over $100 million each in global box office earnings, with five exceeding $500 million each.

Despite over 30 years in the entertainment industry, Smith has maintained a relatively low profile on social media, often leaving his accounts dormant even during film promotions. A notable exception was in December 2021 when Smith appeared on the cover of GQ Magazine. The article, reflecting on his career and his new book, presented a nostalgic look back at Smith's journey since his 20s.

Smith's film debut came with a starring role in *Independence Day*, followed by *Men in Black, I, Robot, I Am Legend, Hancock*, and many others. These roles solidified his status as a box office powerhouse. In 2007, his performance in *The Pursuit of Happyness* earned him his first Academy Award nomination for Best Actor. In addition to acting, Smith has shown a keen interest in film production, with many of his well-known films produced through his production company, Overbrook Entertainment.

Breakthrough with *Independence Day*

Following the success of *Bad Boys*, Smith landed a series of action roles, including his pivotal part in *Independence Day* (1996). Initially little known outside the studio, *Independence Day* became a massive summer hit, establishing Smith as a major movie star. The film opened at number one at the box office, grossing over $104 million in its first week. It quickly became the highest-grossing film of its time, earning over $817.4 million internationally and $306.2 million domestically, with a final global haul surpassing $1.1 billion.

Smith's breakout role in *Independence Day* earned him the National Board of Review's Breakthrough Performance of the Year and his first Saturn Award. The success of the film solidified his status in Hollywood, with media outlets like The Guardian later describing Smith as the "greatest movie star on earth." Smith's newfound stardom was widely recognized, with predictions and advertisements highlighting his rise to superstardom.

Success in Action Films

Though *Ali* (2001) was a significant role, it was Smith's performance in *Independence Day* that truly catapulted him into Hollywood's A-list. This was followed by a string of successful films, further reinforcing his status. Smith showcased his versatility in various roles, proving his prowess as a leading man. His role in *Men in Black* (1997) was particularly notable, with the film becoming the highest-grossing film globally that year.

Movies like *Enemy of the State*, *I, Robot*, *I Am Legend*, *Hancock*, and *Gemini Man* solidified Smith's position as one of the top action heroes of his time. *Men in Black* was especially iconic, with Smith's portrayal of Agent J alongside Tommy Lee Jones as Agent K becoming a cultural touchstone. The film's success spawned a trilogy and received rave reviews for its wit, humor, and special effects.

Exploring Different Genres

With a string of action hits to his name, Will Smith could easily have stuck with the genre that made him a box office titan. However, Smith has consistently demonstrated his versatility by delving into dramatic roles. He starred as Robert Neville, the last man on Earth, in *I Am Legend*; delivered an Oscar-nominated performance alongside his son Jaden in *The Pursuit of Happyness*; and portrayed yet another historical figure in the civil rights drama *Ali*. While Smith has maintained a strong presence in action films, he has also explored comedy, such as with the third entry in Michael Bay's *Bad Boys* franchise, *Bad Boys for Life*, and ventured into the type of big-budget whimsy previously associated with Tom Hanks, seen in *Men in Black* and the family-friendly *Independence Day*.

In the 21st century, Smith has moved beyond merely proving himself at the box office and has sought to diversify his resume. He notably ventured into romantic comedies, a genre that enjoyed significant box office success prior to the rise of comic book movies and Disney blockbusters. Smith's first foray into this genre was with 2005's *Hitch*, where he played a no-nonsense dating coach opposite Kevin James. Despite initial negative reviews, *Hitch* became a rare rom-com hit, grossing $368 million at the box office. This critical and commercial success marked a solid transition for Smith, though he continued to return to action genres where he is best known.

Dramatic Roles

After expanding the movie star business, Smith sought to be taken seriously as an actor. He moved away from the formula of small budgets and solid returns to take on roles that challenged his persona and showcased his natural charisma and emotional depth. In *Ali* (2001), directed by Michael Mann, Smith was put to the test when asked to recreate one of the greatest shows on Earth. Smith's portrayal of Muhammad Ali demonstrated his command and ability to embody a living legend.

Reflecting on this role, Smith once told *The New York Times Magazine*, "I didn't know if I would be able to be convincing in a dramatic role if the rock weren't Dwayne Johnson. But Michael Mann said, 'I think you can do this,' and that was everything for me at that time." This sentiment underscored his belief in storytelling as a unifying force.

Over the past decade, Smith's career has been marked by attempts to reinvent himself, often resulting in mixed success. Despite setbacks, Smith's commitment to evolving as an actor remains evident. His journey underscores the challenges and rewards of pursuing reinvention in Hollywood.

Comedy and Romantic Comedies

Much of Will Smith's comedic work falls within the comedy or romantic comedy genres, despite his prowess in action films. Smith's entry into the film industry was through comedy, and he even starred in a comedy television series before transitioning to film. Romantic comedies often feature an odd-couple dynamic, with characters thrown together in unlikely circumstances that lead to comedic conflict and eventual resolution.

Smith's ability to convincingly portray a variety of roles extends to his work in romantic comedies. His early days as the Fresh Prince showcased his talent for humor, which he carried over to the silver screen. *Bad Boys* (1995) helped transition him to a film career, combining comedy and action in a way that has become a hallmark of his collaborations with director Michael Bay. Smith's aptitude for comedy and the larger-than-life persona he cultivated on *The Fresh Prince of Bel-Air* laid the foundation for his success in romantic comedies.

CHAPTER 4

Behind the Scenes

Although Willard Carroll Smith often appears superhuman, even he cannot escape the passage of time. Smith's role as a producer has evolved significantly. Initially, he co-founded Overbrook Films with James Lassiter, producing notable films such as *Ali* and *Concussion*, in which he starred. Over time, his role has transitioned to that of a versatile producer, evidenced by his work on *The Pursuit of Happyness*. Smith has also produced films like *The Secret Life of Bees*, *Seven Pounds* (in which he also starred), and *After Earth* (starring alongside his son, Jaden). Venturing into directing, Smith worked on *Harlem Nights* and even directed an episode of *The Fresh Prince of Bel-Air* and an hour-long UPN special called *The Star Maker*.

Smith has recently brokered a deal with Hillman Grad Productions, co-founded by Lena Waithe and Rishi Rajani. Established in 2014, Hillman Grad focuses on inclusive storytelling, especially in the horror genre. This partnership follows their collaboration on the true crime documentary *Women of the Movement*, which recently debuted on ABC. Smith's extensive collaboration with director Michael Bay includes eight films, from *Bad Boys* (1995) to *Bad Boys for Life*, and iconic titles like *Independence Day*, *Aladdin*, *I Am Legend*, and *The Pursuit of Happyness*.

Producing and Directing

Recognizing the current demand for family programming, Smith is producing a Nick at Nite series that will blend Broadway-style sitcom recreations with clips and trivia from the network's extensive library. Set to air around Thanksgiving and Christmas, Smith explained in an interview, "It's based on the kids who I have on my record label. I was thinking about shows that are on TV now, and I remember being a kid and not having anything to see me onstage. Now I'd like to show some color. I'd like to have one of those shows where everyone can just stare at the screen, from the parent to the kid."

In addition, Smith has signed a deal with Warner Bros. to develop, produce, and star in an action-adventure movie based on the 1970s TV series *The Wild, Wild West*. He also plans to star in a contemporary action comedy with Jamie Foxx. In 1997, Smith made his directorial debut with Columbia's *Onyx*. Directed by Sanaa Hamri, Will Smith, and Jonathan Mosley, and edited by Happy.ativo, *Onyx* is a gritty mystery thriller about a refugee father from Sierra Leone searching for his daughter in America. The film, lacking flashy effects, aims to provide a deep, thematic narrative. "There's nothing magical about the film—no flashy things or transforming cars—and the ending is sweated out," Smith said.

Philanthropy and Activism

Although his film work slowed after *After Earth*, Smith remained active in public life. His children, Jaden and Willow, followed in their parents' footsteps, achieving significant success in music and television. Will Smith continued acting and dedicated himself to philanthropic endeavors. In 2007, he donated $1.3 million to organizations working to end human trafficking.

Smith's activism began around 1996, influenced by Maya Angelou. He joined several boards, donated to charities, and worked to eradicate gender-based violence. The Will and Jada Smith Family Foundation is a cornerstone of his philanthropic efforts, recently donating 1,000 eco-friendly survival kits to homeless shelters and safe houses. Smith emphasizes the importance of action over publicity and instills these values in his children by involving them in community service.

CHAPTER 5

Personal Life

Will Smith has experienced both the highs and lows of family life, reflecting his dynamic and multifaceted career. He has been married twice; first to Sheree Zampino in 1992, with whom he had a son, Willard Christopher Smith III (Trey), before divorcing in 1995. Smith's second marriage, to Jada Koren Pinkett, began in 1997. Together, they have two children: Jaden Christopher Syre Smith, born in 1998, and Willow Camille Reign Smith, born in 2000. Both Jaden and Willow have followed their parents into the entertainment industry, with Jaden becoming an actor and Willow a singer, rapper, and actress. Jada, a multifaceted artist herself, fronted the metal band Wicked Wisdom from 2002 to 2006 and has acted in notable films such as *The Nutty Professor II: The Klumps* (2000) and *The Matrix Reloaded* (2003).

Trey, Smith's first-born son, opted not to pursue a career in entertainment, which reportedly caused some tension during his upbringing. Will has openly discussed their rocky relationship and the steps they took to repair it, particularly noting a breakthrough moment during the filming of *Suicide Squad*. Will emphasizes that, despite his wealth, his children were not raised with a sense of entitlement, instilling values of hard work and perseverance.

In a 2018 interview with Tidal's Rap Radar podcast, Will candidly discussed the challenges in his marriage to Jada, noting her unconventional views on relationships influenced by her upbringing. The Smith family has also faced financial difficulties, notably being defrauded of $5 million by their accountant. In 2012, the U.S. Government enlisted Will and Willow to help promote the Affordable Care Act, leveraging their influence among young people. This period highlighted the Smith family's commitment to social and political causes, despite personal differences in some of their views.

Marriage and Family

When not on set, Will Smith is dedicated to spending time with Jada and their children, Jaden and Willow. Navigating the pressures and long hours of the entertainment industry, Will and Jada have managed to maintain a solid foundation in their marriage, unified by their shared passion for family and entrepreneurial endeavors.

Will and Jada strive to be actively involved in their children's lives, even before their entrance into the industry. Reflecting on Jaden's first film, *The Pursuit of Happyness*, Jada remarked, "At the end of the day, when you devote yourself to children and don't compromise your career, it's really important that if I can't be on his set to be with him, his father can." Will echoed this sentiment, noting Jaden's impressive work ethic and the irony of his young son's eagerness to work.

Will's personal reasons for starring in *The Pursuit of Happyness* were deeply intertwined with his family values. "There are very few films that my kids will watch, and I'm in the damn movie," he quipped, underscoring his desire to create meaningful work that resonates with his family.

Challenges and Triumphs

Will Smith's journey has been marked by both challenges and triumphs, attributing his successes to perseverance and resilience.

Despite his outward charm and comedic talent, Smith faced significant hardships, from financial struggles to personal setbacks. Born on September 25, 1968, Smith's path to success was not straightforward, especially after his father, Willard Carroll Smith Sr., left the family when Will was just 13.

Finding solace in music and rapping, Smith eventually transitioned to acting, creating a foundation of financial stability for his family. However, his journey wasn't without its low points. In a 2007 interview with *60 Minutes*, Smith recalled a period when he was broke: "I was out of money... I didn't buy anything for three years. Everyone was saying, 'this kid is at the end.' Now, people would say, 'he's just getting started!'"

Smith's story is a testament to his determination to overcome adversity and continue evolving, both personally and professionally.

CHAPTER 6

Legacy and Influence

Will Smith's career has had a profound cultural impact, making it challenging to measure his legacy in its entirety. He began as a sitcom sensation, conquered the music world, and ultimately became one of the most enduring and versatile movie stars of his time. One of Smith's most notable contributions to the industry is his advocacy for diversity in Hollywood. In 2020, The Public Theater of New York City named Smith number two on their list of the "Greatest Stage Stars of the Past 25 Years," based on responses from over 300 industry professionals regarding performances over the past quarter-century.

Smith's work has left a lasting impression on audiences. His words and actions resonate long after the lights come up. For instance, he once told *Ebony* magazine, "Build a fallout shelter out of steel and concrete in your mind... And when every man is hating and discriminating against your origin, skin color, or religion, I want you to take your goodness and keep arriving." This sentiment, from the film *Shark Tale*, reflects the optimism and resilience that Smith embodies, whether he's acting or simply addressing the public.

Impact on Diversity in Hollywood

Will Smith has played a crucial role in advocating for diversity in Hollywood. In the 1990s and 2000s, seeing black talent top the charts wasn't entirely uncommon, but these actors and filmmakers often had to contend with and subvert historically reductive labels and stereotypes. Smith has consistently used his prominence to challenge the status quo and promote inclusion. In a 2001 letter to the industry, he called out the lack of diversity among top grossing producers, actors, and directors, asking, "Where are the people of color?"

Smith continues to advocate for diversity and inclusion in Hollywood. He has used his influence to support A-list films and ensembles across the racial spectrum and has highlighted the work of emerging black talents. For example, he brought together Jonathan Majors and Zazie Beetz for the film *The 40-Year-Old Version* with Radha Blank. Smith's company, Westbrook, acquired *King Richard*, considered one of the best films of 2021, for $60 million. Smith's early Oscar win was seen as a major accomplishment for both Hollywood and the black community. His ongoing efforts indicate that he is far from finished, continuing to forge new opportunities and challenge the industry.

Inspirational Quotes and Memorable Moments

Will Smith has shared many inspirational quotes and memorable moments throughout his career. Here are a few:

- "You can do any and everything you want. You can live the life of your dreams. You have to roll up your sleeves. Help others. Be of service to others. Your heart points to the answer and to the life of your dreams."
- "Whether it's solitary confinement or just playing against the odds, I'm gonna love from any place. I'm gonna love under any circumstance."
- "Your conception determines your perception. How you were conceived, how you were born, determines how you view

your beginnings in life. You are destiny. Your life is a work of art."

One of the most famous moments from his career occurred in *The Fresh Prince of Bel-Air*. In a powerful scene from the first episode of the fourth season, Smith's character breaks down while thinking about his real father who had left him. This moving moment showcased Smith's acting talent and earned him significant acclaim. It was a pivotal episode that helped ensure Smith's lasting success and financial stability.

Conclusion

In this paper, we examined the transformation of Will Smith from a street-savvy, homegrown Philadelphian, known as "The Fresh Prince," into a polyvalent cultural commodity and Hollywood royalty. We sought to understand the symbiotic relationship between this individual transformation and broader shifts in the rap industry, the television industry, and American culture.

Smith's evolution from a street-smart Philly kid to a Hollywood superstar mirrors the trajectory of rap music, which has evolved from an ignored and marginalized form of expression into a respected and mainstream genre. This transition is emblematic of the broader cultural legitimation of black music, allowing it to transcend racial boundaries and contribute to the self-expression of a diverse audience.

In Western liberal democracies, where freedom of consumption often determines social freedom, Smith's journey from television to blockbuster films exemplifies the revitalizing impact of the "hip-hop renaissance" on surrounding culture industries. Some might attempt to reverse engineer this argument to theorize about individual hip-hop artists' escape from negative stereotypes. Will Smith, having always been perceived as socially "white" in terms of neighborhood and class, used his persona to bridge gaps and challenge social norms without being pigeonholed into negative stereotypes.

While it is not our intention to universalize this narrative, Smith's story is a crucial formation in understanding how hip-hop rose above the ignominy of the U.S. "inner city nightmare" and the deindustrialization of the nation. This transformation has had significant effects on Smith himself, the youth of America, and the culture industries at large.

Smith's career is a testament to the power of reinvention, resilience, and the ability to challenge and change cultural narratives. His influence extends beyond the screen and the stage, impacting social perceptions and paving the way for future generations of artists and entertainers.